FIRST IMPRESSIONS

FIRST IMPRESSIONS

REMBRANDT

GARY SCHWARTZ

HARRY N. ABRAMS, INC., PUBLISHERS

SERIES EDITOR: Robert Morton
EDITOR: Ellyn Childs Allison
DESIGNER: Joan Lockhart
PHOTO RESEARCH: Lauren Boucher

LIBRARY OF CONGRESS CATALOGING-IN-PUBLICATION DATA

Schwartz, Gary, 1940–
Rembrandt / Gary Schwartz.
p.   cm.—(First impressions)
Includes index.
Summary: Surveys the life and work of the well-known seventeenth-century
Dutch artist and discusses the reasons for the rise and fall of artists' reputations.
ISBN 0–8109–3760–3
1. Rembrandt Harmenszoon van Rijn, 1606–1669—Juvenile literature.
2. Artists—Netherlands—Biography—Juvenile literature.
[1. Rembrandt Harmenszoon van Rijn. 1606–1669.   2. Artists.
3. Painting, Dutch.   4. Art appreciation.]   I. Title.   II. Series:
First impressions (New York, N.Y.)
N6953.R4S437   1992
759.9492—dc20
[B]   91–26171   CIP   AC

CHAPTER ONE

THE CROWN OF FAME

istory does not call many people by their first names. Famous men and women who aren't kings, queens, or popes, bishops, knights, or noblewomen go into the history books very formally. Eleanor Roosevelt didn't need her last name when she was alive, and George Bernard Shaw was GBS, but their nicknames are not enough anymore. To be known to history by your first name, you have to be more than just famous. You have to be a hero to generations after you, nearly a god on earth. Such a man was the Dutch artist Rembrandt.

What Rembrandt is famous for are the paintings, prints, and drawings he made more than three hundred years ago. His reputation was established by the time he was twenty-five years old, about 1630. From then on his fame spread. Today he is known to hundreds of millions of people in all parts of the world.

Individuals as outstanding and important as that can never be understood completely. The facts of their lives tend to get mixed up with legends. Sometimes they themselves help the legends get started. For example, it was Rembrandt who began calling himself by his first name only. His full

Self-Portrait. 1632

About 1630, in his mid-twenties, Rembrandt made more than a dozen little self-portrait etchings. They are among his most delightful prints.

name was Rembrandt Harmensz. van Rijn. This brings to mind a story about another first-name immortal, Napoleon. At his formal coronation as emperor of France, people said that he seized the crown from the pope and crowned himself. In a way, Rembrandt took the crown of fame out of the hands of his contemporaries and put it on his own head.

Great artists are hard to understand for another reason as well. We are interested in them because of their art. But we cannot always be certain whether a particular work of art is by the master or not. Hundreds of paintings and drawings that are considered original Rembrandts by some experts are doubted by others. And even when they all accept a work as a genuine Rembrandt, chances are they have different opinions concerning its meaning or quality.

In other words, no one can tell you exactly why Rembrandt is a great artist or what makes a certain work by him great. What I will try to do in this book is to present clearly the most important facts, as I see them, about his life and his art.

For the illustrations, I have chosen only works accepted by all present-day Rembrandt experts. But the facts and the illustrations do not speak for themselves. If you want them to help you understand why Rembrandt is so exceptional, you will have to think about them. You will have to compare his life story with the lives of other people from the past and present, and compare his art with the art of other painters. Your image of Rembrandt as a person and an artist will therefore depend on how much you know, how you feel about things, and how you draw your comparisons.

Most of all, you will have to use your imagination. In the chapters on Rembrandt's life and career, try to picture his situation in the various stages he went through. In the discussions of his art, try to let the illustrations convince you that you are seeing the subjects they show: seventeenth-century Dutch people, landscapes of real places, Bible scenes, and even angels and God himself. Look at them closely and tell yourself what you see and feel. Doing this together with a friend may help you put your impressions into words.

It is not known if this old woman really was Rembrandt's mother, but if so, his mother was one of his top models. He drew, etched, and painted her constantly in Leiden.

Rembrandt was out to create pictures that could come to life in our imagination. Each of us can make them live. And even if we cannot find the words to explain to one another what makes Rembrandt remarkable, we can, if we are honest, form a judgment for ourselves and have fun while doing it.

CHAPTER TWO

❧

BECOMING AN ARTIST

O n July 15, 1606, Rembrandt was born as the ninth child (there were to be ten) of a well-to-do couple in Holland in the city of Leiden. His father's name was Harmen, so he was called Rembrandt, Harmen's son. In Dutch, this second name comes out as Harmenszoon, usually shortened to Harmensz. That way of naming was a Dutch practice from a time when no one used family names. If a man named Jan had a son Peter, the boy would be Peter Jansz. A daughter Elizabeth would be Elizabeth Jansdr. (Jan's daughter). Since Jan is a common name, you would not be able to tell from their names alone that Peter and Elizabeth were brother and sister. By 1606 Rembrandt's father did have a family name: Van Rijn,

The Windmill. 1641. **Rembrandt's father's mill, similar to this one in Amsterdam, was located on the city wall in Leiden.**

meaning "from the Rhine." In fact, the family house overlooked the Rhine River where it enters Leiden. A few steps from the front door, on the city wall, was a windmill owned by Harmen van Rijn. When Rembrandt looked out of the window, he saw his father's mill and beyond it the Rhine River and the countryside of a part of Holland known as the Rhineland. It must have given him a strong feeling of being where he belonged.

Most people in Leiden were poor and had no work, so Rembrandt was fortunate to grow up in a family with a good income. The source of that income was the mill. Farmers from the surrounding area would bring malt there to be ground and sold to brewers in the city. In good times, the mill could support the family of the miller and his hired hands. Two of Rembrandt's older brothers worked with their father in the mill and another became a baker, like Rembrandt's grandfather on his mother's side. The family did not have all the luck in the world. Harmen and his oldest son were partly crippled by accidents with guns. They had been drafted into the Leiden civic guard, a kind of citizens' army, and both of them, at different times, had injured their hands firing their weapons. This must have made it hard for them to do the heavy work in the mill.

Harmen and his wife, Neeltje, sent their sons to school. The daughters, like their mother and two out of every three girls of their generation, never learned to read or write. We know this because they signed legal documents with a mark rather than a signature. The older boys probably did not stay in school beyond the age of ten, but when Rembrandt finished his basic education at about that age, his parents allowed him to go on to high school. The school they sent him to was the best in Leiden, the municipal Latin School, from which a boy—no girls were admitted—could graduate at the age of thirteen or fourteen and go on to the university. Rembrandt's first biographer tells us that his parents hoped he would get a job with the city government. But in his final year he was taken out of school. This may have been for purely personal reasons. According to the biographer, Rembrandt loved painting and drawing so much that he pestered his parents to let him train to become a painter.

There is another possible reason why Rembrandt's parents put aside the idea of a civil-service career for him. It was a complicated one, having to do with religion and politics. Until the century before Rembrandt lived, almost all Christians in Europe were Catholics. In the sixteenth century, Protestantism came into being as a challenge to Catholicism. Within Protestantism, there were further splits, resulting in sects such as the Lutherans, the Calvinists, and the Mennonites. Twenty years before Rembrandt was born, the Calvinists had replaced the Catholics as rulers of the northern Netherlands, where Leiden was. (In the southern Netherlands, the opposite happened, and the Catholics kept all the power.) During Rembrandt's high-school days, another revolution occurred. This time the strict Calvinists forced the moderate Calvinists out of office and out of most government jobs. Although Rembrandt's father was a strict Calvinist, the family included many Catholics and moderate Calvinists, so Rembrandt's chances of getting ahead in the civil service were not very great. The removal of moderate Calvinists even extended to his school, where the assistant principal was dismissed. These events suggest that Rembrandt was taken out of school to avoid conflict with the authorities.

With his school career behind him, at about the age of thirteen Rembrandt was sent to a painter as an apprentice, or working pupil. At that time, people we consider artists—painters, printmakers, sculptors—were usually thought of as craftsmen. They were subject to the same rules applied to other professionals, such as weavers, brewers, or surgeons.

The painter to whom Rembrandt was apprenticed was Jacob Isaacsz. van Swanenburgh. His father had been burgomaster (mayor) of Leiden in the moderate Calvinist party. Van Swanenburgh had an adventurous past. About the age of twenty, he moved to Italy, where he married a Catholic girl and raised a family. He kept this secret from his parents. Only after his father's death did he move back to Leiden, in 1615.

If Rembrandt's daydreams about being an artist were like those of other boys his age, we can picture him drawing faces, figures, and animals out of his head, while fantasizing about painting for the prince of Orange or the Holy Roman Emperor. But his new circumstances must soon have brought him down to earth. From a noisy schoolroom and a household with ten children, he entered a quiet, serious one-man studio. In his late forties, Van Swanenburgh must have looked like an old man to the thirteen-year-old Rembrandt. The master's wife may have learned some Dutch in the four years she had been in Holland, but she and her husband certainly spoke Italian at home. It must have been a strange time for Rembrandt. As for the apprenticeship: if Rembrandt's father was at all a typical Dutch miller, his parting words to Van Swanenburgh after putting Rembrandt in his care would have been, "Work the boy hard."

An apprentice to a painter *did* work hard. He was not just a pupil. Much of the time he did studio chores—grinding pigments, mixing fluids, stretching canvases, sanding oak panels,

Pieter Lastman. *Odysseus and Nausicaä.* 1619. The story of this painting is from Homer's ancient Greek epic poem, the *Odyssey.* It tells how Odysseus, after the Trojan War, wandered from country to country for ten years before he was allowed by the gods to return home. On the island of Scheria his boat was wrecked. There the king's daughter, Nausicaä, and her father rescued him. Lastman fills the scene with color and fun.

14

brushing in layers of neutral paint to prepare a canvas or panel for the master, running errands, and cleaning up. If the boy's father paid well enough, the master would take time to give instruction. Since painters were not trained teachers, the quality of their lessons depended on their gifts for explaining their craft.

As for the atmosphere in the studio, there are plenty of stories about Dutch painters who were always drunk, who beat and insulted their apprentices, or who refused to teach them, cheated them, or locked them up. Jacob Isaacsz. van Swanenburgh was not as bad as that. A relative of his wrote in a family chronicle that he was very good-natured. He taught Rembrandt the fundamentals of art. The basic technique for learning was copying. An apprentice would copy models like plaster casts of parts of the human body, stuffed animals, drawings and paintings by the master, and engravings of the work of other artists. One of the most important parts of the training, and the hardest for young artists, was learning to take their inspiration from art rather than their own imaginations.

After spending several years with Van Swanenburgh, Rembrandt went to Amsterdam to complete his apprenticeship in the studio of another Dutch artist who had been to Italy, Pieter Lastman. Lastman painted subjects of many kinds, such as landscapes, still lifes, and portraits. His main specialty was "history painting": narratives from the Bible, the mythology of classical Greece and Rome, and ancient, medieval, and modern history. In order to succeed at this work, an artist had to command many different skills. Like every painter, he had to be able to create the illusion of three-dimensional space on a flat surface, a technique known as perspective. In addition, he had to know the stories he painted and all the characters in them. He had to be familiar with earlier artists' representations of the same subjects. And to bring his scenes to life convincingly, a painter had to give each figure an appropriate expression, pose, and costume. His scenes had to be placed against a background of landscape or architecture. They had to be decorated with modern or antique objects and colored in harmonious or contrasting tones. To do this well required much knowledge and good taste. All of it was part of Rembrandt's training.

There was a lot to learn and it left the teenage Rembrandt little time to develop a style of his own as an artist. But that was not expected of him. Apprentices learned to paint exactly like their masters. The highest compliment that could be paid to a young artist was to say that no one could see the difference between his work and that of his master. Even after apprenticeship, most painters tried to imitate the style of an established artist. There were good reasons for this. Works of art were made to be sold, and the more closely they resembled works for which there was a market the easier they were to sell. Most buyers did not know very much about art. They felt safe if the work of a beginner looked like that of an artist they knew.

Because of this, a beginning painter did not usually become an independent master right away. Typically, he would first work in the studio of his master or another artist, producing paintings in his style. That way he could earn a steady income and save money toward opening a studio of his own. In the meanwhile, he could show his work to well-wishers among his family and friends. Not until an artist had his own customers and patrons did it make sense for him to develop an individual style. And even then, most painters found it wise not to stray too far off the beaten track.

Rembrandt was no exception to that rule. When he completed his training, he did not take the risk of working on his own. He joined up with another young Leiden painter, Jan Lievens. Lievens too had gone to Amsterdam to study with Lastman, some years before Rembrandt. The information we have, which is not complete, indicates that Rembrandt and Lievens shared a studio, and that the work they produced was sold by Lievens's father. The two young painters, still in their teens, practiced the specialties they had learned from Lastman. Lievens painted portraits as well. Together they made quite an impression. Thanks to their training with Lastman, they had a more sophisticated style than most painters in Leiden. They tackled complicated subjects, which demonstrated a high level of knowledge. Not everyone could appreciate such art. The viewer too had to have considerable education to understand it.

Rembrandt and Lievens worked long hours every day, trying out new techniques not only in painting but also in printmaking. They copied the work of Lastman, the famous painter from the southern Netherlands Peter Paul Rubens, and other artists they admired. They even copied each other. Rembrandt and Lievens were the talk of Leiden by their early twenties. Their reputation spread to The Hague, to the court of the prince of Orange, and by 1629 at the latest they had begun working for him, for much more money than they had been earning. While still living at home, within ten years after leaving high school, Rembrandt was a success.

Rembrandt's career had a lot going for it: he had more money than most of his colleagues, a superior education and training, excellent connections, lots of self-confidence, a generous measure of intelligence and talent, ideas of his own about art, and ambition and daring.

What he did not have, as we shall see, was the ability to take charge of his own life. He earned much money but ended up losing it; he had a classical education but did not like to put it to use; few of his connections with people who advanced his career lasted very long; his self-confidence came across to most people as arrogance. His ideas about art were strong and personal but not clear: scholars are still debating what they were. He used his daring not only to break through barriers in art but also to get his way with people, sometimes very unreasonably. With a personality as complicated as that, it is no wonder that Rembrandt's life was full of ups and downs. He created a great stir, became a model for many younger artists, and created works that have moved millions of people. But he also brought a lot of unhappiness to people close to him and caused confusion in the world of art during his life and after his death.

CHAPTER THREE

REMBRANDT'S BREAKTHROUGH

rederick Henry, prince of Orange, count of Nassau, count of Katzenellenbogen, count of Vianen, marquess of Veere, etc., was a very busy man. He was the most important person in a dynamic young country, the United Provinces (there were seven), also known as the Dutch Republic. In 1584, when Frederick Henry was born, the country had just been formed. Until five years before his birth, the Seven Provinces were not independent. They were part of the seventeen Netherlandish provinces belonging to the king of Spain, Philip II. Frederick Henry's father, William of Orange, was the leading nobleman of the Seventeen Provinces. He took his title from the small princedom of Orange in the south of France, but his real power was in the Netherlands. When the nobility and the city governments of the Netherlands got into a conflict with the king of Spain, they turned to William for help. He tried to keep all parties together but did not succeed. In 1579 the seven northern provinces—Holland, Zeeland, Utrecht, Gelderland, Groningen, Fries-

Self-Portrait. About 1629. Several European
princes and kings collected portraits of famous people and
self-portraits of important artists. Charles I of England owned
a self-portrait of Rembrandt; this is probably it.

Gerard van Honthorst, Rembrandt's contemporary, painted the important leader of the Dutch Republic Frederick Henry in 1631.

land, and Overijssel—formed a government of their own: the States General. William went with them. His official title remained the same: *stadholder,* or deputy. But he meant more than that to the Dutch. They called him the Father of the Country.

He was also the father of eight daughters and four sons. Frederick Henry was the youngest of them all. When he was six months old, his father was assassinated by an agent of Philip II. In time, Frederick Henry's older brother Maurice became stadholder. When he died, in 1625, Frederick Henry succeeded him.

What kept Frederick Henry busiest was his work as commander in chief of the armed forces. The Dutch Republic was at war with Spain, which was not as far away as it might seem. The southern Netherlands still belonged to Spain, and territory on the long border between north and

A year later
Rembrandt portrayed
Frederick Henry's wife,
Amalia van Solms.

south was being lost and won all the time. Frederick Henry's strength as a general was siege warfare. He knew how to surround a city, choke its supply lines, and await its surrender. This was less heroic than fighting pitched battles, but it was less bloody, and the Dutch admired him for it.

Being a prince and leader of an important country like the United Provinces brought more responsibilities than military ones alone. Frederick Henry's father and brother had raised his family to great prominence, and it was up to him to make sure it stayed there. It helped that his cousin was king of Denmark and that he was related by marriage to the king of England. But this was also embarrassing, since his own position was not royal at all. Being prince of Orange was little more than a formality, since Orange was surrounded by France, and Frederick Henry was never even able to visit it. His position as stadholder of the Dutch Republic was an appointment by the States General. After years of lobbying, Frederick Henry succeeded in having the title turned into a hereditary dignity that he could pass on to his son. (You may want to know how the House of Orange did in the long run. Not badly. With some interruptions, succeeding generations remained stadholders of the Dutch Republic until it ended, in 1795. And since 1815, when the northern Netherlands became a monarchy, they have been its kings and queens. Today the country is ruled by Queen Beatrix of Orange-Nassau, countess of Vianen, marchioness of Veere, etc.)

Frederick Henry was obliged by his status to live well. How could he expect people to take him seriously as a prince if he did not have a palace or two and if those palaces were not furnished in princely style? The House of Orange did own several palaces, but most of them were located inconveniently outside the Dutch Republic, some even in enemy territory. Frederick Henry had no choice but to build some of his own. Because he did not have time to supervise the construction and decoration himself, he hired people to do it for him. One was his assistant secretary, a young man by the name of Constantine Huygens, who was to play an important role in Rembrandt's career.

Constantine's father had been secretary to Frederick Henry's father. When Constantine was a small boy, his father took him along on a diplomatic trip to the south, when the Twelve Year Truce of 1609 made that possible. As he tells us himself, he charmed everyone in sight with his drawing, improvised poetry, and music-making. "Everyone loves a child prodigy," he wrote candidly in his autobiography. Some of his friends were surprised when Constantine accepted a job as assistant secretary to Frederick Henry. Was this enough of a challenge for someone who knew his languages and literature so well that he could write letters and even poems in Latin, English, French, German, Italian, and Spanish—not to mention his native language, in which it is not easy to write well? Constantine was one of the great Dutch poets of all time. He played the lute like a professional, wrote hundreds of musical compositions, and was able to draw and cast medals and design buildings. Constantine himself did not think that these talents would be wasted in the service of the prince of Orange. In fact, by making the most of them, he eventually became chief secretary and was able to arrange for his son — also named Constantine — to become secretary to Frederick Henry's grandson.

When Constantine was in the field with Frederick Henry on a military campaign, he would entertain him by discussing books on architecture. What the two men admired above all was the classical building style of ancient Greece and Rome, which had been revived in Italy during the Renaissance. It was only natural that when they agreed about the superior quality of one or another model in a book, Frederick Henry would ask Constantine to have something of the kind built for him. Constantine

Thomas de Keyser.
Constantine Huygens. 1627.
This is the man who admired young Rembrandt and helped him at the court of the prince of Orange.

Rembrandt made this
etching after a Rubens
self-portrait in 1630 and painted
himself in a similar way
the following year.

looked for architects who shared the same ideas, and formed a circle of sculptors, carpenters, masons, bricklayers, and gardeners. At a time when most building in the republic still followed time-honored Dutch forms, the palaces of Frederick Henry looked like Italian villas and the new classical palaces of the kings of France, England, and Denmark. In this way, Constantine helped Frederick Henry to distinguish himself. The style and size of his palaces put him in a class with European royalty.

Decorating the prince's houses was a challenge of the same kind. The furniture, woodwork, lamps, tapestries, and paintings had to be fit for a classical palace. In Holland it was difficult to find artists and artisans with the ability to produce work of that kind. The artist Constantine most wanted to employ was Peter Paul Rubens, who had designed tapestries and produced grand paintings for royalty all over Europe. Rubens knew Latin and corresponded with scholars as an equal. He collected ancient art and built a classical house and garden for himself. All of this can be seen in his paintings. The figures stand in the poses of ancient statues and are grouped the way they would be in classical scenes.

Other artists from the southern Netherlands did come to work for

Frederick Henry, but not Rubens. The reason was not artistic but political. Rubens was so prominent and capable that he was given a high rank at the court of the king of Spain. On his travels, he performed diplomatic missions, perhaps even espionage, for the archenemy of the Dutch Republic. This made it impossible for the chief official of the republic to honor him with commissions.

Constantine went in search of a Dutch artist with the gift of creating classical art. When he saw the work of Rembrandt, he became convinced that he had found him.

Rembrandt was in his early twenties when Constantine Huygens discovered him. He was working in Leiden, mostly for local collectors who were not willing to spend very much money on art. The usual price for a painting was in the neighborhood of ten guilders. That was enough to pay for renting a room and eating simple food for a month. Etchings and engravings printed on paper went for half a guilder. This was a far cry from the kind of money being earned by the great Rubens. Depending on the size and complexity of a painting, Rubens charged from five hundred to thirty-five hundred guilders for a single canvas.

While Rembrandt's work was attracting attention and praise, there were those who had their doubts about it. The first written notice we have concerning him is an entry made in 1628 in the diary of a man who followed the Dutch art world very closely, Arnoldus Buchelius. He wrote, "The Leiden miller's son is being praised highly, but prematurely." In other words, Buchelius thought it was too early to tell whether Rembrandt was going to fulfill his promise. Within a year or two, Rembrandt was to be put on a pedestal as one of the greatest artists of his time and was to start earning money on a scale he could only have dreamed of until then.

At the time, Rembrandt was still very close to Jan Lievens. Constantine

The Repentant Judas. 1629. Constantine Huygens compared this painting to the art of the ancient Greeks, although to our eyes there is no resemblance. To understand what he meant, read the text nearby.

was tremendously impressed with both of them. "Never have I come across such hard work and dedication," he wrote, adding that the quality of their art was little short of miraculous, considering that they were mere commoners and had mediocre teachers. Of Rembrandt, Constantine wrote that he "captured for the Netherlands the prize of artistic excellence from Greece and Italy." To us, Rembrandt's paintings do not look anything at all like Greek or Italian art. Why did Constantine compare them?

His meaning becomes clearer when he describes one painting in detail, *The Repentant Judas Returning the Thirty Pieces of Silver to the Chief Priests and Elders.* Judas had been one of Christ's apostles. He betrayed Christ for a bribe and felt so guilty about it afterward that he committed suicide. The painting shows him in deep agony. He has come back to the Jewish priests who bribed him, hoping to relieve his guilt by giving back the money. He has thrown the coins on the ground, at the feet of the officials. His twisted pose demonstrates without words how sorry he was. When Constantine says that in this figure Rembrandt combines individual and universal features better than any Greek painter could, we begin to understand what he means. A Greek artist wishing to show a figure in agony would use a standard set of poses, gestures, and expressions from older art. Such a figure would be recognized by Greek viewers as a formula for regret. Rembrandt does something else, according to Huygens. He observed the actual physical effects of profound emotion on individual human beings, and used those for his Judas. Therefore, Rem-

This engraving was made in about 1610 from a drawing of *The Repentant Saint Peter* by Abraham Bloemaert. Rembrandt used this print as a model for his figure of Judas shown on the preceding pages and in the detail opposite.

brandt's painting can be seen both as the story of the biblical sinner Judas and as a study of a human being trying to atone for an unforgivable sin.

In writing down his thoughts on the painting, Huygens performed a great service for us. Very few Dutch art lovers of Rembrandt's time took the trouble to put into words what they felt about art. Between the lines, Constantine tells us what was important to him about Dutch art: accurate observation, emotional power, and the ability to make one model stand for all of humanity. These are qualities for which Rembrandt's art is still praised today.

What Constantine did not know is that Rembrandt's Judas was not really taken directly from life. The young painter had been practicing for years on twisted figures with clenched fists, copying examples by other artists, and trying to improve on them. This does not mean that his version was any less good than Constantine said it was. But it reminds us that a good artist can convince anyone that art is more like life than it actually is.

Constantine also tells something about Rembrandt and Lievens as persons. In appearance they were young for their age, but they behaved like a pair of old men. They were so serious that they never went out just to have fun. Because they worked all day sitting or standing still, they were not very strong, and he worried about their health. They were exceptionally intelligent but annoying to talk to, since they thought they knew it all. The reader of Constantine's autobiography can almost hear the arguments between the young artists and the prince's secretary, only ten years older than they. Rembrandt's classical education came in handy at such moments. Not many Dutch artists knew Latin. Constantine must have been impressed.

Having found two such promising young artists, Constantine began showering them with orders for paintings for the prince of Orange and his court. The legendary story of Rembrandt's first sale of a painting in The Hague fills us in on some other aspects of his personality. He received a hundred guilders, ten times his usual rate. He treated himself to an expensive coach ride back to Leiden, rather than take the barge, which was

slower and cheaper. He was so nervous about having so much cash on him that he was afraid to leave the coach when it stopped at a wayside inn. While the driver and the other passengers were inside, the horses broke loose and carried Rembrandt to Leiden on their own. He left without paying, doubly pleased to be home quicker than otherwise, and for free.

There is no way to know whether or not this really happened, but Rembrandt's conduct in the story is in character with much that we know about him from more reliable sources: he was keen on earning lots of money, liked to live luxuriously, and was not more scrupulous in financial affairs than he had to be.

Apart from the money, Rembrandt's work for the prince brought him other advantages. His work came to the attention of important people. For example, a self-portrait by Rembrandt was given to an English ambassador, who in turn gave it to the king of England. At court, Rembrandt came into contact with people who knew a lot about art and artists, and he was able to talk to them about his work. He found out which other painters were admired at court and did his best to study examples of their art. Naturally enough, Rembrandt tried to see whether he could paint as well as or better than they. Sometimes he was asked to do just that, as when he had to paint a portrait of the wife of the prince to match a portrait of the prince by Gerard van Honthorst (see page 21). Challenges of this kind help an artist to advance by sharpening his self-criticism.

The greatest challenge was to match Rubens. In painting after painting for the prince, Rembrandt adapted compositions by the great master. *The Raising of the Cross* and *The Descent of Christ from the Cross* are based loosely on famous paintings by Rubens in a church in Antwerp. Even a Rembrandt

The Raising of the Cross. About 1633. Rembrandt painted this work for the prince of Orange, and included his own face in the scene to show how pious he was. By doing so he also smuggled a self-portrait into the prince's collection.

31

self-portrait from this period is modeled after one by Rubens. This kind of copying was done by all artists at the time and was not considered cheating. It was a way of measuring yourself against established masters and proving to the outside world that you were as good as they. Rembrandt threw himself into such commissions with body and soul. He was so involved in his work that he painted his own face into *The Raising of the Cross,* as one of the men helping to raise the cross to which Christ is nailed.

Rembrandt's work for the prince of Orange made him one of the best-known artists in the country. Moreover, the prince paid him very, very well—as much as six hundred guilders for a single painting, more money than an average Dutchman earned in a year. But the number of commissions he received from the prince was limited. And what would happen, he must have asked himself, if those commissions were to stop altogether? In his mid-twenties, in the early 1630s, Rembrandt made a move that helped him cash in on his reputation and safeguard his career. He left his home in Leiden for Amsterdam, where there were lots of wealthy people who

Left:
Jacques de Gheyn III. 1632.
Opposite:
Maurits Huygens. 1632
These two portraits are of very good friends. Each owned Rembrandt's picture of the other. When Jacques died, he left the portrait of Maurits to his friend.

bought paintings.

As things turned out, this was a timely change. If you live on income from a prince, and if the prince is under no obligation to continue paying it to you, you have to remain very good at your work, very nice to the prince and his advisers, and very lucky. In Rembrandt's case, this combination worked for five years, and then broke down. What seems to have happened is that Rembrandt lost the support of Constantine Huygens. In 1629, in his memoirs,

Constantine called Rembrandt his friend and the man who brought the glory of Greece to Holland. Four years later, the next time he wrote about the artist, his tone had changed. In eight two-line Latin poems, Constantine found eight sarcastic ways of saying that a portrait by Rembrandt looked nothing like the man who sat for it. There seems to be more to the story than just the truth to life of a painting. The sitter was a childhood friend of Constantine's, and Rembrandt's portrait of him was one of a pair. The other one showed Constantine's own brother. This suggests that something went wrong in the relationship between Rembrandt and Constantine. Rembrandt may have made Constantine jealous somehow. In any case, commissions from the court stopped coming about this time.

In one way, it is a pity that Rembrandt stopped painting for the court. If he had continued, he probably would have had more opportunity to do the kind of work he seemed to like the most: painting stories from the Bible, like *The Repentant Judas*. But the move to Amsterdam did not damage his career. In fact, it helped him become richer and more famous than ever.

CHAPTER FOUR

SUCCESS IN THE BIG CITY

msterdam in the 1630s was one of the great cities of the western world. It was the main European center of shipping and overseas trade. The harbor was called a "forest of masts" because countless sailing ships from all over the world were anchored there at any given time. Amsterdam businessmen controlled much of the traffic in grain from Poland, Russia, and the Ukraine. Their companies had a monopoly on trade with the East and West Indies, Japan, Brazil, and New Netherland (later New York). The canals of Amsterdam were lined with warehouses for storing goods.

Such vast sums of money changed hands on a daily basis that it was impractical to deal in cash. A bank was needed to keep track of the traders' accounts. That way, payments could be made just by subtracting a number from one account and adding it to another. To make sure this was done honestly, the city itself opened a bank. Traders also wanted to buy shares in each other's ventures. For this purpose a stock exchange was founded. The Amsterdam bank and stock exchange were the most reliable anywhere.

A View of Amsterdam. About 1640. Although he always lived in cities, Rembrandt almost never depicted them. This is the only skyline of Amsterdam among his etchings.

Above: *Saint Jerome.* 1648. Rembrandt devoted seven etchings to Saint Jerome including this unfinished one. The hermit-scholar is always shown with his tame lion, studying or praying in a cave or other lonely spot.

Right: *The Three Trees.* 1643. For Rembrandt, even the quiet countryside on the outskirts of Amsterdam expressed the drama of nature.

Rembrandt made m

the

Rembrandt f. 1648.

...ore than forty little etchings like these showing only beggars and
homeless. He used such figures in the sidelines
of his paintings from the Bible and history.

They made it possible for people to do business just by exchanging checks and shares instead of moving actual goods or even coins. Once this system was working, it attracted investors from all over Europe. They made Amsterdam the biggest money market in the world.

The wealthiest Amsterdam families ran the town government. They prided themselves on being more than mere merchants, using their fortunes and power for the good of society at large. They improved living conditions by adding large new areas to the old city. The new university they started was open to professors and students of different religions. (Leiden University, by contrast, was dominated by Calvinists.) Mostly, however, they used their power to increase their profits, and they spent their profits on themselves. Although the government passed laws limiting the open display of wealth, splendid new houses arose in the city and the country, decorated with expensive furnishings and works of art. Calvinist preachers told their congregations to dress simply, and maybe they did on Sunday when they went to church. But styles became more and more luxurious. The most expensive jewelry from all over Europe found its way to the grand houses on the new canals: the Prince's Canal, the Emperor's Canal, and, most glorious of all, the Gentlemen's Canal. Amsterdam was a boomtown.

Among the most wanted luxury items were paintings. From all over the northern and southern Netherlands and beyond, artists moved to Amsterdam to fill the demand. Rembrandt was one of them. Another was a painter and art dealer named Hendrick Uylenburgh, who took over an art shop in the same street where Rembrandt had lived when he was an

∾

Christ Preaching (The Hundred Guilder Print). 1643–49.
This famous etching combines different sayings of Christ into one
scene in a way no artist had ever done before.

apprentice to Pieter Lastman and where quite a few other artists had their studios: the Breestraat (Broadway). It was located in a new area, and it was much wider and brighter than the streets in the older part of the city.

With loans from private investors, Uylenburgh began a lively trade in painting single portraits and group portraits, buying, selling, and cleaning paintings, publishing and selling prints, and exploring every other way there was of earning money in art. One of the investors was Rembrandt, who in the spring of 1631 put one thousand guilders into Uylenburgh's business. Not long thereafter, Rembrandt moved in with Uylenburgh on the Breestraat.

Rembrandt was more than a lodger in Uylenburgh's house. He became the manager of his studio as well. He trained apprentices, who painted copies of compositions by Rembrandt.

Uylenburgh was able to provide Rembrandt with lots of well-paid commissions. One of the first was a group portrait of eight Amsterdam surgeons. Paintings of this kind were very popular in the northern Netherlands. Most of them show minor officials, like the board members of organizations. Almost every respectable Dutchman belonged to an organization (called a guild) of all the people in his line of work, or to a civic-guard company, or to the board of a charity. These bodies had an official purpose, but they held social get-togethers as well. The citizens who belonged to these organizations came from the same clans that also controlled government and trade. They could afford to pay for portraits. Once an organization owned one group portrait, later officers were tempted to add another.

The Amsterdam surgeons' guild already had three group portraits when Rembrandt was asked to paint a fourth. The older paintings showed guild lecturers teaching anatomy to other surgeons, and Rembrandt also took this as his theme. The lecturer was a man named Nicolaes Tulp, a member of the town council and future burgomaster of Amsterdam. His

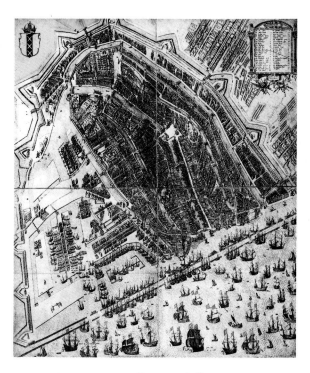

In this map of Amsterdam, east is to the left of the city's center. Rembrandt first lived on that side and then moved across town, to the west.

status explains why he was able to get a corpse to dissect. This was not an easy thing to do, as it is in medical schools today. No normal Dutch citizen would leave his body to science. Only the corpses of executed criminals were put on the dissecting table, and to obtain them took a special court ruling. When permission was granted, the surgeons still had to wait and see if the weather would be cold enough on the day of the criminal's execution to preserve the body for an extra day or two. Demonstrations like the one shown in the painting did not take place more than once every two or three years.

As we might expect, given his training as a painter of stories, Rembrandt decided to show the anatomy lecture as a dramatic event. He borrowed the tense poses and attentive expressions of the four listeners closest to the corpse from a Rubens painting of a completely different subject, *Christ and the Tribute Money*. This helped Rembrandt to make the point that anatomy had a religious as well as a scientific meaning. The working of the human body was a sign of God's wisdom, and dissection was a way of revealing it.

Peter Paul Rubens. *Christ and the Tribute Money.* 1610–15.
The arrangement of the figures and some of the poses in this painting
of a story from the life of Christ were borrowed by Rembrandt
for his first group portrait.

Rembrandt's painting brought this out more clearly than the other paintings of anatomy lectures, and the surgeons seem to have valued it highly.

The Anatomy Lecture of Dr. Nicolaes Tulp is the kind of painting you can look at for a long time, admiring its lifelikeness. It also gives you a lot to talk about. It makes you think about the art of portraiture and the practice of surgery and medicine in Holland. You wonder what it was like to be standing so close to a corpse and what Dr. Tulp is saying to his attentive audience. It also inspires you to contemplate death and the meaning of life.

Two modern scholars, one an art historian and the other a historian of science, have each written an entire book about this painting alone. In Rembrandt's time, it was certainly the subject of much admiration and discussion.

Perhaps most important of all for Rembrandt's career, it hung in a place where it could be seen by many people. There was no such thing as a public museum in the seventeenth century. For an artist to become widely known, good paintings by him had to hang in places that were visited by many

The Anatomy Lecture of Dr. Nicolaes Tulp. 1632. **The corpse from Rembrandt's painting of Dr. Tulp can easily be inserted into Rubens's group scene shown opposite. This is not just a trick; it shows how much Rembrandt was influenced by Rubens.**

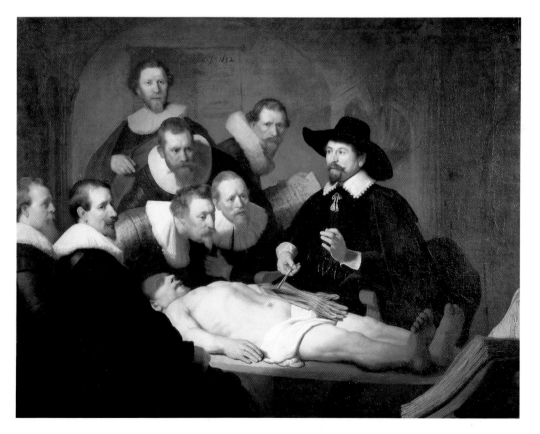

people: a palace, a town hall, a courtroom, or the hall of a guild. Works by Rembrandt were already on display in the prince's gallery in The Hague and the king's gallery outside London. That gave him prestige. The portrait in the surgeons' guild hall in Amsterdam brought in business.

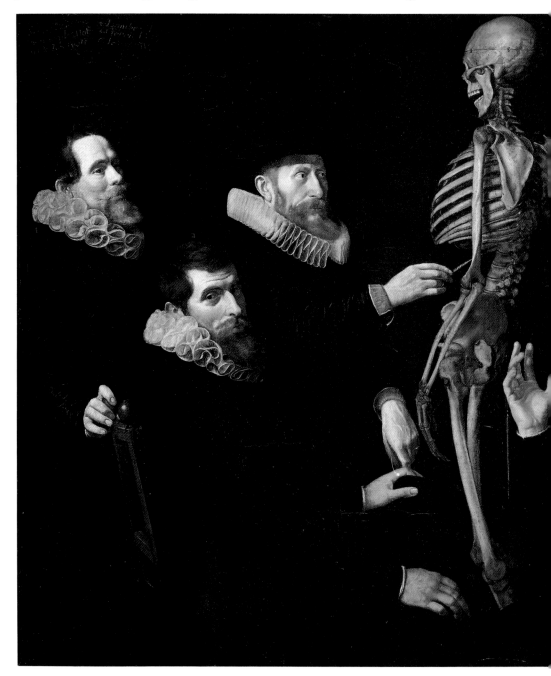

Rembrandt was not slow to capitalize on his fame. In his first two years in Amsterdam, he painted fifty portraits that we know of. Considering the large number of paintings that have disappeared in the course of time, it is not impossible that during those years he painted as many

as two a week. He charged high prices, ranging from fifty guilders for a head to five hundred guilders for a life-size, full-length portrait. At this rate, Rembrandt was able to earn as much in a week painting portraits in Amsterdam as he had earned for a complicated biblical painting for Frederick Henry on which he sometimes worked, on and off, for years. Once again, as when he started painting for the court, Rembrandt's career took a giant leap forward.

∽

Both before and after Rembrandt painted his first anatomy lesson, the surgeons' guild commissioned other group portraits. *The Anatomy Lecture of Dr. Sebastiaen Egbertsz. de Vrij* was painted in 1619, probably by Werner van den Valckert. It is the only one of its kind in which the lecturer works from a skeleton rather than a corpse. This may be because Dr. de Vrij was in political trouble at the time and it may have been difficult for him to get a corpse for dissection.

He became a favorite portrait painter for several groups of Amsterdamers with money. A few of them were Calvinists, like Nicolaes Tulp. But most belonged to other religious groups. This was an important issue for an artist, because religion was not only a matter of personal belief in Europe in the seventeenth century. It was also a major factor in politics and economics, as it still is in many parts of the world today. Calvinism was the official religion of the Dutch Republic, and only Calvinists were able to hold political office. Other religions were tolerated, but only as long as they held their services in private houses. Each group tended to stick together, living in the same neighborhoods and doing business with their fellow believers both in Amsterdam and in other places in the Netherlands and abroad. Rembrandt's employer Hendrick Uylenburgh was a Mennonite, a follower of the religious leader Menno Simons. The fact that Rembrandt lived with him and painted portraits of Mennonites, Catholics, and members of a Protestant church called the Remonstrants meant that he could not be completely trusted by strict Calvinists, even though he was a Calvinist himself.

Uylenburgh not only helped Rembrandt's career as a painter. He also wanted Rembrandt to continue making etchings, which he had started to do in Leiden. Etchings are prints made from copper plates on which the artist has drawn a design in a special technique we will discuss later. A painting could only be sold once, but when an artist has made an etching plate, it can be printed many times and the print sold to different customers. Etchings were much cheaper than paintings, so more people could afford them. They were also easier to transport and could help spread the fame of an artist in distant places. For Uylenburgh, Rembrandt made a very large etching called *The Descent of Christ from the Cross*. It reproduces one of Rembrandt's paintings for Frederick Henry and looks a lot like a famous altarpiece by Rubens. In a way, it announced the arrival of Rembrandt as the Dutch Rubens.

The Descent of Christ from the Cross. 1633

Having followed Rembrandt's career until the age of about twenty-eight, we now know how he became so well known. He was presented as a Dutch challenger to the great Rubens by two influential people: Constantine Huygens and Hendrick Uylenburgh. When these important brokers of art commissions adopted an artist, other people noticed and talked about it. And Rembrandt gave them plenty to talk about. His paintings and etchings provided material not only for much enjoyment but also for discussion and debate. His sudden rise to fame and riches, between the ages of twenty-three and twenty-eight, was the most spectacular success story in the Dutch art world. And his personal life, as we shall very soon learn, was always worth following.

∞

Hendrick Uylenburgh had a young cousin named Saskia. She and Rembrandt met and decided to get married. This is not a short version of a long story. It is all we know.

Saskia's branch of the Uylenburgh family were not Mennonites but Calvinists. They lived in Friesland, to the east of Amsterdam, in the provincial capital of Leeuwarden. Saskia's father, who died long before, had been a burgomaster of Leeuwarden. An adviser to William of Orange, he had been the last man to see William alive before his assassination. Saskia was clearly in a higher social class than Rembrandt. By marrying her, Rembrandt gained family ties to individuals more important than his own relatives.

In one respect, the marriage was typical. It was customary for Dutchmen to marry within their professional group. By marrying the cousin of Hendrick Uylenburgh, Rembrandt became related to a major art dealer with whom he already worked very closely. The tie was important for both of them. It also complicated their lives. From 1633 on, Rembrandt was not only an investor in Uylenburgh's business and the supervisor of his studio

Saskia. 1633   *Saskia.* 1634

but also his in-law. Even though Saskia was only destined to live for nine years after the wedding, Rembrandt remained closely linked to the Uylenburghs for the remaining thirty-six years of his life.

The story of Rembrandt and Saskia's marriage is told in four kinds of documents: registries of births and deaths, last wills, court cases, and works of art. The first kind is the saddest. Saskia gave birth to four children, three of whom died before they were two months old. The survivor was the last of the four, a son, Titus. But giving birth to him was too much for Saskia's health. She died six months later, just before she would have turned thirty.

Whether Rembrandt and Saskia were deeply in love we cannot say. It does seem that they had a good time together. Such a good time that a relative of Saskia's in Friesland spread gossip that the couple was wasting

the family fortune. What business was it of his? you may ask. Well, it was. If Saskia had died without children, or if her children died without children, most of the money she had when she married Rembrandt would go back to her family. This was common practice in the Netherlands, and it made for a lot of tension in many families.

Rembrandt's portraits of Saskia show her in different ways. About the time of their marriage, he drew her face in silverpoint, a special technique that produces a delicate line that cannot be changed once it is drawn. This very personal portrait is inscribed by Rembrandt: "My wife when she was 21 years old, the third day after our marriage on June 8, 1633." Saskia wears a big, floppy straw hat with a ribbon of flowers and holds a single bud in her hand. A few years later, Rembrandt painted her as a great lady, dressed in velvet and fur and decked with precious jewels. As unapproachable as she seems, in this painting, too, she touchingly holds a flower or twig in her hand. She seems to be acting a part, rather than sitting for her portrait.

The most spectacular painting of Saskia shows her seated on Rembrandt's lap, looking over her shoulder toward us as he raises a glass of wine, a broad grin on his face. Here as well, the models are playing a part. It has been suggested that Rembrandt is posing as the hero of a Bible story known as "The Prodigal Son." Prodigal means spendthrift, spending lots of money on things a person doesn't need. In the story, one son of a wealthy man leaves home and squanders his share of his father's fortune on wine, women, and good times. When his money runs out, he is reduced to a job feeding pigs in order to stay alive. Swallowing his pride, he returns home, and his overjoyed father prepares a feast. The other son, who has stayed at home and listened to his father all along, is furious. But the father tells him it is right to celebrate, since his brother "was dead, and is alive; he was lost,

❧

Rembrandt and Saskia. **About 1636**

55

and is found." The moral of the story is that it is never too late to repent, or to forgive.

It was not unusual for portrait sitters, or artists painting self-portraits, to be shown as actors in a Bible story. People in those days looked for their role models mainly in the Bible. But why would Rembrandt want to depict himself as an unrepentant sinner and his wife as a loose woman? And why would he do it at a time when his wife's family was accusing the young couple of being prodigals themselves? We have no answers to these questions. Perhaps this is one of those stories that you cannot understand unless you were there at the time.

Rembrandt did not take the gossip lying down. He sued Saskia's relative, claiming that he and his wife were blessed with "superabundant wealth (for which they cannot be thankful enough to the Lord)" and had no need of Saskia's inheritance to live as well as they did. He lost the case, but his

&

Rembrandt's house in the Breestraat in Amsterdam is today a museum in which nearly all of the artist's etchings are on display.

Cornelis Claesz. Anslo and Aeltje Gerritsdr. Schouten. 1641.
In this double portrait of a married couple, as in his larger group
portraits, Rembrandt aimed for tension and action.

∽

claim was true enough at the time. Rembrandt was the most successful
artist in Amsterdam, and his earnings showed it.

He and Saskia lived in rented rooms for a few years after their marriage.
In 1639 they bought a large, expensive house in the Breestraat, a few doors
from where Uylenburgh lived. Rembrandt did not have enough cash to pay
for the house, so he took out a mortgage. It was a big loan, but not too big
for him to repay in installments, given his excellent income at that time.

Unfortunately for him, he did not keep up his payments on the mortgage—with disastrous results, which we will find out about in a while.

The kind of painting that brought in the most money for the time spent on it was the portrait, and that is what Rembrandt concentrated on for the first few years of his marriage. Most profitable were double portraits of husband and wife, and it is interesting to study the example seen on page 57, especially since we have just looked at a double portrait of Rembrandt and Saskia.

The subjects are the Mennonite preacher Cornelis Claesz. Anslo and his wife, Aeltje Gerritsdr. Schouten, painted in 1641. The Mennonites did not have paid clergymen. Any member of the community could preach, and all were expected to earn their own living. Anslo was in the textile business, grain and lumber trade with the Baltic countries, and shipping. He was quite wealthy. He could have asked Rembrandt to paint him in his office, with a view of his ships in the harbor of Amsterdam, but he preferred to have himself shown in his study, "speaking to his wife about the Bible lying open before him on a table. She, depicted with incomparable art, listens to him attentively and with visible concentration." The quotation is from a note about the painting written a hundred years later by a great-grandson of Cornelis and Aeltje who still owned the double portrait.

The famous Dutch poet Joost van den Vondel wrote this poem about the painting:

> Aye, Rembrandt, paint Cornelis' voice!
> His visible self is second choice.
> The invisible can only be known through the word.
> For Anslo to be seen, he must be heard.

The quotation and the poem make us look at the painting in a certain way. In the figure of Aeltje, we look for "visible concentration," and in that of

The Risen Christ Appearing to
Mary Magdalene. 1638

Cornelis for an invisible voice. Aeltje's pose and facial expression do suggest concentration. With her head turned at a slight angle, she gazes intently at nothing in particular, her left hand clenching her kerchief. Cornelis leans toward her, his lips parted and his hand extended the way it would if he were making a point while talking to her. Our imagination is challenged to provide the missing element that binds the two figures: the sound of Cornelis's voice. Although we do not hear it, we are sure that this is a painting of a man talking to a woman about something serious. Clues to what he is saying are provided by the open book, which seems to be a Bible, and by the candlestick with one candle, not burning. This detail looks important, like an object standing for something else. But we are no longer sure what it symbolized.

A few years before, Rembrandt painted another kind of dialogue between a man and a woman: the Bible scene of Christ in the form of a gardener appearing after his death to Mary Magdalene. The body of the Magdalene is turned toward the tomb where Christ was buried after the Crucifixion, but her head is twisted toward the risen God. The poet Jeremias de Decker, who saw Rembrandt painting the picture, later put the action into these words:

> Christ seems to say "Marie, don't tremble, I am here,
> It's me. Your master's free of Death's authority."
> Believing, though not yet with all her heart and mind, she
> Seems poised between her joy and grief, her hope and fear.

De Decker praises Rembrandt for illustrating the scene from the Gospel of Saint John as faithfully as can be done in paint. Like Cornelis Anslo's gesture, this too is a way of bridging the gap between word and image. But interpretation is a lot easier when you know the text, and when you have a witness who saw the painter at work.

CHAPTER FIVE

❧

INTERPRETING PICTURES

In discussing the paintings of Rembrandt and Saskia and of Cornelis and Aeltje we come face-to-face with a tremendous problem in the study of art. Both pictures look as though they have a particular meaning. At first sight, we think we understand what they are saying. But when we try to put the meaning into words, we only get so far and no further. Sometimes we come close, as with the Anslos, and sometimes we stay frustratingly distant, as with Rembrandt and Saskia.

Art historians have different ways of dealing with this problem. Some ignore it, saying that the only things that matter about art are qualities that cannot be put into words.

Those who do try to interpret images usually begin by comparing representations of traditional themes with each other and with texts from literature and religion. This is known as *iconography*. Iconographers discuss the theme of *Rembrandt and Saskia*. Is it or is it not "The Prodigal Son in the Tavern"? When they have the answer to that question, they will feel that the problem is solved.

Other interpreters will not be satisfied at that point. They say: "This is a painting of a man with a woman on his lap, with a peacock pie in the background. The costumes, gestures, and facial expressions all have their own meanings." They look at the painting as a set of signs and try to puzzle out what each sign means, and how all of them work together in the painting.

Another school of art historians

stresses the point that every interpretation is linked to a certain time and place in history. My generation has very different ideas about art than the Europeans and Americans who lived in the 1890s, when Impressionism was an important style of painting. Rembrandt's contemporaries are even further away from us in time and in outlook. Scholars of this school prefer to study what the artist's contemporaries said about works, rather than stand behind their own interpretation.

Those who take the last standpoint to its extreme deny that any interpretation is truer than any other. They claim that everyone who looks at a painting interprets it in his or her own way, no matter what tradition or the history of signs says. If that is so, a work of art cannot be said to have any fixed meaning at all. It only has the meaning we ourselves give it. Such a meaning is valid only for us, and sometimes only for one moment in our lives. Not even the idea of Rembrandt concerning the meaning of a work of his own can be said to be truer than what the work means to you, today.

Each of these methods of interpreting artworks has produced important insights into the meaning of art. But none of them have been adopted by all art historians. Most books on art mix them together to produce a method that makes sense to the writer. When you read a book on art, you should try to figure out where the writer stands on the question of interpretation. This is not always easy. Many writers think that *their* method is so sensible that no one could possibly disagree with them and therefore do not find it necessary to explain themselves.

My own approach combines visual interpretation with historical reconstruction. To my mind, the meaning of a work is not in its appearance alone. Unless we know what it meant to the artist and to the people he made it for, we miss an important part of its meaning.

Take the painting of Cornelis Anslo and Aeltje Schouten, for example. From documents in the Amsterdam archives, we know that Cornelis was the preacher of the Mennonite congregation to which Hendrick Uylenburgh belonged. We also know that

Hendrick borrowed a large sum of money from the church in 1641, the year the portrait was painted. As security for the loan, he gave the church 125 etching plates, which must have included Rembrandts.

These facts may have had an effect on the appearance of the double portrait. They could have led to the decision to portray Anslo as a preacher rather than a merchant. It is not unlikely that Uylenburgh was the one to suggest that Rembrandt paint Anslo, and that he paid part of the fee in gratitude for the loan from Anslo's church. In that case, the large format of the painting, and perhaps its very existence, came about as a result of the loan. But even if the background circumstances had no influence at all on the appearance of the portrait, they certainly were a part of the picture's meaning to Anslo, to Rembrandt, and to Uylenburgh. The poet Vondel was probably involved as well. He was a relative of Uylenburgh's, and had other close ties to the Amsterdam art world.

The creation of this portrait, in other words, was probably part of a complex financial, business, and family transaction. Even if the painting had different meanings to each of the individuals involved, still there was a common understanding of why it was made and for whom, and why it was made the way it was. This is what I would call its original meaning. It involves all aspects of the origins of the work: the identity and status of the artist and of the person, institution, or market for which it was made; the subject, iconography, style, quality, and price; the personal, social, and religious connections between all concerned; the use to which the finished work was put; and what was said about it by those who first saw it. It is certainly no easier to reconstruct this meaning than to interpret a picture on the basis of its appearance alone. But interpretations of the first kind are the ideal toward which I strive as an art historian. Even if the documents needed to prove such an interpretation are missing, I try to form in my mind an idea, based on whatever *is* known about art in that period, which includes as many of the above considerations as possible.

CHAPTER SIX

✤

MID-LIFE

embrandt was so satisfied with his invention of a "speaking hand" in the portrait of Cornelis Anslo that he used it again the next year in the largest and most ambitious portrait commission of his career. Frans Banning Cocq, who strides forward in the center of the painting, gestures with his left hand as he speaks to a subordinate. In his family album, a sketch of the painting is given this caption: "The Young Lord of Purmerland, as Captain, Ordering His Lieutenant, the Lord of Vlaardingen, to Let His Civic Guard March Out." The world knows the portrait better by the incorrect title *The Night Watch*.

Rembrandt was asked to paint *The Night Watch* by a company of Amsterdam civic guardsmen. The members were not soldiers but civilians, or burghers, who bore arms in defense of the city. There were twenty burgher companies in Amsterdam. Each held target practice, meetings, and social get-togethers at one of three halls: one for the crossbowmen, one for the archers, and one for the musketeers. The guardsmen in *The Night Watch* were musketeers (the musket was an early type of rifle), and they met at the Musketeers' Practice Range, or Kloveniersdoelen. It was located

✤

A detail of *The Night Watch* showing Frans Banning Cocq at center.

in Precinct II, where Rembrandt and most of his customers lived.

The painting was made for a new meeting hall added to the building in the mid-1630s. All the practice ranges were decorated with group portraits of burgher companies, and it was logical for the musketeers to order some new paintings of this kind for their new hall. But they decided to do something that never had been done before in Amsterdam: to have group portraits made of all six musket companies.

The portraits were painted by the most famous artists in Amsterdam. As each painting was completed and hung, it was certainly compared with the others. We cannot listen over the shoulders of the musketeers as they judged *The Night Watch* against the group portrait by Rembrandt's former pupil Govert Flinck, for example, or the one by the distinguished German painter Joachim von Sandrart. The best source we have for the reactions people had at the time to the paintings are some remarks put into a book thirty years later by another former pupil of Rembrandt's, Samuel van Hoogstraten. It is worthwhile to read them carefully while looking at *The Night Watch*.

It is not enough for a painter to put his figures next to each other in rows. One sees all too much of that here in Holland in the civic-guard halls. True masters succeed in unifying the entire work. . . . Rembrandt observed this principle in his painting in the guard hall in Amsterdam extremely well. Some say he did it too well, over-emphasizing the big picture in his imagination at the expense of the particular images he was commissioned to paint. In my opinion, though, Rembrandt's painting, however deserving of criticism it may be, will outlast all its competitors. It is so painterly in conception, so elegantly posed, and so powerful that some people feel that all the other portraits in the hall look like playing cards next to it. I would have liked to see him illuminate it with more light, though.

The Night Watch. 1642. The guardsmen in this painting are not on watch and the scene does not take place at night. But the picture has become so famous with this title that there is no way to correct the mistake. Art historians still argue about the real subject of the work. If they ever agree, perhaps they will convince the rest of the world to change the title.

∽

There is a lot to think about in those words. They give enough arguments pro and con to reconstruct an authentic seventeenth-century discussion on the merits and defects of Rembrandt's art. One of the most intriguing remarks is the contrast between the "big picture" in the artist's imagination and the individual images in the scene. Some of his contemporaries apparently thought that Rembrandt had too much imagination for the good of his art. *The Night Watch* (page 67) is presently hung in the Rijksmuseum in Amsterdam together with the other group portraits from the hall of the Kloveniersdoelen. If you ever visit the Rijksmuseum, you can pretend to be a Dutch musketeer and choose the artist you would best like to paint your portrait.

In 1642 Rembrandt's luck changed for the worse personally, financially, and professionally. On June 14 of that year, he lost Saskia. She left him with the nine-month-old Titus. Ten days before she died, she rewrote her will, leaving everything she owned to Titus or, under certain circumstances, to her sisters in Friesland. From that moment on, Saskia's relatives kept an even closer watch on Rembrandt than during his marriage, checking to make sure he wasn't losing or giving away Titus's inheritance. In fact, Rembrandt did give away part of the inheritance and lost much of the rest, so Titus ended up with only a small portion of what was due to him.

Even if Rembrandt had been financially successful from then on, virtually every move he made for the remaining twenty-seven years of his life would have created problems for him with the Uylenburghs and the courts. But after 1642, he never again earned enough for his needs, which made matters much worse. With each passing year, his chances to repay the mortgage on his house and his debt to Titus diminished, and the financial noose around his neck tightened.

His personal life became a nightmare. Saskia gone, Rembrandt had a love affair with the nurse who came into his house to take care of Titus, a young widow from Edam named Geertge Dircx. He gave her gifts of jewelry, including some pieces that had belonged to Saskia. After a few years, though, Rembrandt fell in love with another woman, Hendrickje Stoffels. Realizing that he could get into trouble with the Uylenburghs for having given away some of Saskia's jewelry, he tried to get it back from Geertge. She wrote a will leaving most of what she owned, including the jewelry, to Titus, but she also tried to get Rembrandt to marry her. When he refused, she took him to court. He ignored two summonses, and when he appeared at the third hearing, he said, "The lady claims I slept with her? Let her prove it!"

The court believed Geertge without proof, and although it did not go as far as to order Rembrandt to marry her, it did order him to pay her two hundred guilders a year for support. The fight turned very ugly, and at a given point Rembrandt conspired with Geertge's brother to have her put away in a penal institution. She was given a twelve-year term. After five years, some old friends of hers from Edam found out what had happened and were able to have her released, in spite of Rembrandt's threats and protests. The trouble started all over again, but Geertge died within half a year, and that was that, except for a new fight between Rembrandt and Geertge's brother, which also went to court. The brother, a seagoing man, claimed that Rembrandt was harassing him. The artist had asked for him to be arrested on the day his ship was due to sail.

This is a terrible story, and it has created disagreement among art historians. Some, like myself, interpret it to mean that Rembrandt had a streak of unreliability and vengefulness that could take extreme forms. His behavior, as we know it from other legal documents as well, was often nasty and untrusting, leading him into more conflicts than any other Dutch painter we know. This fits with the opinions about his character written by some of the people who were acquainted with him.

Hendrickje Bathing. 1655

Other scholars are unwilling to believe such a thing of an artist who could create such tender and understanding pictures of human beings as did Rembrandt. They argue that we should not judge the behavior of someone long dead without knowing more about the facts of the case. (My reply to this is that there are more documents about Rembrandt and Geertge than about any other aspect of his life.)

The connection between the character of an artist and the nature of his or her art is not that simple. The author of *Winnie-the-Pooh*, A. A. Milne, brought pleasure to millions of children, but made the life of his own son miserable. On the stage and in recordings, Elvis Presley stood for the traditional values and pleasures of the red-blooded country boy, but in his life he was a criminal abuser of drugs and girls. Rembrandt was, I believe, a case of this kind. His images of Christian faith and human love have moved millions of people for hundreds of years. Somewhere inside, he had instinctive contact with these feelings. He may have wanted to live his life

Young Woman in Bed. About 1647. The model for this painting was probably Geertge Dircx, who lived with Rembrandt for about seven years.

according to them, but he didn't. Does this change the meaning of his art for us? Sometimes it does and sometimes it doesn't. When we look at a painting like the *Young Woman in Bed* and realize that it may be Geertge just before Rembrandt fell out of love with her, it takes great effort to enjoy it without thinking of the fate in store for the model at the hands of the artist.

About 1642 Rembrandt's temper got him into serious trouble professionally as well. He had painted a large, expensive portrait of Frans Banning Cocq's brother-in-law, a man named Andries de Graeff. De Graeff was a powerful man in Amsterdam, with the kind of connections that could make or break a career. He was vain and stingy, and in his dealings with Rembrandt he lived up to his reputation. For some reason or other, he refused to pay the agreed-upon fee of five hundred guilders for his

Andries de Graeff. 1639. **This man and Frans Banning Cocq were brothers-in-law in one of the most powerful families in Amsterdam. Rembrandt painted brilliant portraits of them but after he finished the second one nobody in the family ever gave him another commission.**

Jan Six. 1647

portrait. Rembrandt, instead of compromising quietly, sued de Graeff. He won the case and got his money, but lost the backing of de Graeff and his family. All the other painters who worked on the group portraits in the musketeers' meeting hall were given new work in later years by the captains they painted or their families. All except Rembrandt. For more than ten years after 1642, he painted no more group portraits and no more portraits of any of the wealthy Amsterdamers whose business had been his main source of income. He never regained financial stability or his peace of mind.

The first Amsterdam patrician to give Rembrandt work after *The Night Watch* was Jan Six. A wealthy man who did not have to work for a living,

Six's Bridge. 1645. According to legend,
Rembrandt won a bet by making this etching in the time
it took a servant to fetch a pot of mustard
from a nearby village.

Six spent his time and money on art, books, and the theater. He wrote plays himself and helped other playwrights get produced and published.

When an artist works for someone who is not sure of his own taste, or for the open market, he or she is better off sticking to traditional, accepted forms of art. But Six, like Constantine Huygens, was a connoisseur: a judge of quality in art. Sophisticated patrons or customers such as these like to be surprised with something new, so the artist can experiment. The first piece of work Six commissioned from Rembrandt was an etched portrait. It shows the patrician in an unusually informal pose, leaning casually in a windowsill, reading. The books and manuscripts on the chair in the foreground and the painting on the wall identify Six as a lover of literature and art. The saber on the table suggests an interest in fencing. The technique of the etching, with its many shades of black, is very refined, showing the artist to be a virtuoso in his craft.

As in his portrait of Cornelis Anslo and Aeltje Schouten, here Rembrandt tries to capture in a picture something invisible: not the sitter's voice but his mind. If you look closely at the etching, you will notice a certain peculiarity in the lighting. The part of Six's face turned away from the window would normally be in shadow. In the portrait it is lit, not directly, but by light reflected from the open page. Symbolically, this tells us that Six's mind is illuminated by his intellectual efforts. A poem on the etching by the theater publisher Jacob Lescaille reinforces this interpretation. The title says that Six is shown "in his library, practicing the learned sciences," and begins: "Behold Jan Six, as he refreshes his soul by diligently searching out, in books, the core of wisdom." This draws the viewer into the sitter's inner world: we are curious to know what he is reading and thinking, just as we would like to know what Anslo is saying and how his wife is reacting to it.

Another etching by Rembrandt linked to Jan Six is a landscape traditionally known as *Six's Bridge*. If the portrait etching of Six can be called a composition in black, the landscape is an equally virtuoso scene in white, making maximum use of the sheet of paper itself as background. Six gave Rembrandt still more opportunities to display his wizardry: in drawings, a frame design, an illustration for a printed play by Six, and most spectacularly in a painted portrait of the patrician. The painting combines two different styles, roughly comparable to the black and white modes of the two etchings. The sitter's face and hair are dense and detailed, while the hands and garments are dashed off with as few brushstrokes as possible. Yet, the overall effect of the painting is perfectly unified.

A little poem by Jan Six on a portrait of his brother Pieter tells us something about how he looked at art:

The painter is quite pleased; he's managed to express
The inner Pieter Six by means of outwardness.
His giving nature shows in golden-yellow hair
And purity of soul in features white and fair.

The painting of Jan Six pleased not only the sitter, but also his descendants. Ten generations later, the portrait is still owned by the family.

Through Jan Six, Rembrandt's contacts in the theatrical world, which were already considerable, took on new meaning. Playwrights who were being helped by Six and fellow patricians who served on the theater board, began working with Rembrandt. In this way, Rembrandt began once more to get commissions from Amsterdam officials. The same thing happened in the medical world. In the 1650s, Six married the daughter of Dr. Nicolaes Tulp, who by then had risen to the rank of burgomaster. This connection helped Rembrandt get a commission for a group portrait of surgeons and for portraits of individual physicians. Thanks to the protec-

During the period when Rembrandt was working for Jan Six, shown at left in a portrait from 1654, he received a commission for the group portrait opposite. The painting exists now only in this fragment, having been badly damaged in a fire.

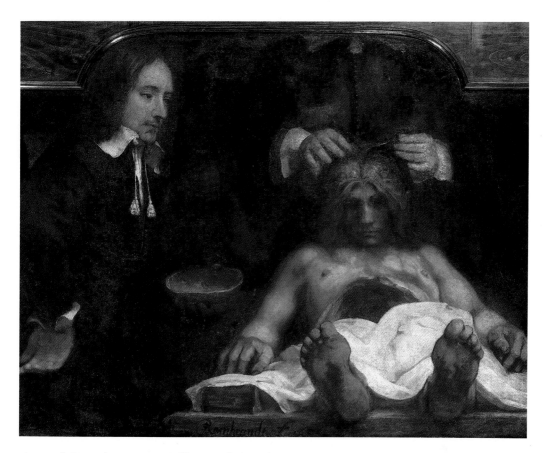

tion of Six, the worst effects of Rembrandt's fight with Andries de Graeff were finally being overcome. By then Rembrandt was fifty years old.

Unfortunately for both men, Rembrandt was not able to keep the friendship of Jan Six. The breakup came about 1656 and had to do with money. We know of two transactions that went wrong. One was a loan from Six of a thousand guilders, which neither Rembrandt nor his cosigner was able to repay. The other had to do with a contract concerning the purchase by Six of three paintings from Rembrandt. When a disagreement arose over the terms of the contract, Rembrandt claimed to have lost the document. The details are unknown, but they were unpleasant enough so that the painter and his patron never worked together again. We can only dream about what might have been had Six and Rembrandt continued to stimulate each other.

CHAPTER SEVEN

✑

THE LAST YEARS

y the time he fell out with Six, Rembrandt's entire life was in a shambles. In 1652, when the Dutch Republic went to war with England and everybody in the country needed cash, the people who had lent Rembrandt the money to buy his house started to put serious pressure on him to pay them back. For a few years he was able to keep the moneylenders happy with small sums and promises, while doing what he could to protect himself should their demands become too pressing. Some of the measures he took were not legal, and they got Rembrandt into fresh trouble. In one last effort to raise cash, he hired a hall for a three-day auction of most of what he owned, probably including a lot of his own work and that of other artists. The proceeds were not enough, and in any case he did not use the money to pay off any of his old debts. This must have been the last straw for his creditors.

In the end, bankruptcy was inevitable. Between 1656 and 1660, the courts sold all of Rembrandt's possessions, including his house, at a series of auctions for the benefit of the creditors. Most of them had to settle for a fraction of what they had lent to Rembrandt. This painful arrangement did

✑

Titus van Rijn. 1655. **Rembrandt shows his thirteen-year-old son at work.**

not release Rembrandt from all the claims that might be brought against him. For further protection, he took shelter behind Hendrickje, who lived with him as his common-law wife, and his son Titus. Rembrandt had them form a company dealing in art, for which they were entirely responsible. He worked for the firm as an adviser, in exchange for a liberal allowance. Everything he painted became the property of the firm, not of the painter, so it could not be seized by people to whom Rembrandt owed money. This was humiliating for Rembrandt and dangerous for Titus and Hendrickje.

Titus became Rembrandt's pupil, specializing in paintings of still life and animals. He was a well-meaning boy and tried to help his father, but that was more than he — or anyone else — could do. Once he found himself in the office of a Leiden publisher who needed an engraved portrait to

Jan Antonides van der Linden. No one knows why, but Rembrandt made this portrait as an etching when the publisher who ordered it had specifically asked for an engraving, an entirely different technique.

The Conspiracy of Claudius Civilis. 1661–62. The new town hall of Amsterdam was decorated with scenes from the Roman period of Dutch history. This is all that remains of Rembrandt's contribution, which was taken down after only six months.

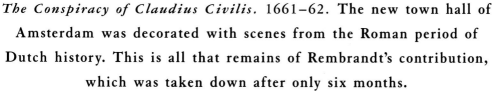

illustrate a book. This kind of print is made by cutting grooves into a sheet of copper with a sharp wedge called a burin. When the grooves are filled with ink and passed through a press with a sheet of paper covering the plate, the ink is forced onto the paper to leave a printed impression. Titus knew that Rembrandt owned burins, although he used them only for special effects on etchings. Etchings are printed in the same way as engravings, but the grooves are made differently — not by a cutting instrument, but by acid, which bites into the plate through a layer of wax in which the artist sketches the subject with a needle. Etching plates produce fewer impressions than engravings before they wear out. Rembrandt was famous

Self-Portrait. 1661–62. Many explanations have been given for the circles in the background, but art historians still do not agree on their meaning. In any case, Rembrandt is shown at his most appealing.

for his etchings, and the publisher asked Titus if he could, for once, make an engraving. Titus said, "Are you kidding? My father can engrave with the best of them." The publisher gave him the commission, but when Rembrandt delivered the portrait, it was etched and not engraved. It was refused by the publisher, and poor Titus had to swallow his shame.

Rembrandt had one more great opportunity in his last years to restore his reputation. He was invited by the burgomasters of Amsterdam to paint a huge canvas for the new town hall. The ground-floor corridors were decorated with scenes of the revolt of the early inhabitants of the northern Netherlands, the Batavians, against the Roman army that occupied their country. Rembrandt's assignment was to paint Claudius Civilis, a fierce, one-eyed Batavian leader, making a solemn oath to expel the foreigners. His painting hung in the town hall only for half a year before it was removed, for reasons unknown to us, and returned to the artist, unpaid for. He cut it down to the central subject, in which form it still survives as an impressive fragment.

Rembrandt's last years could not have been sadder. When he was fifty-seven, Hendrickje Stoffels died in a plague, only thirty-seven years old. She left him a daughter named Cornelia. Rembrandt was sixty-one when Titus was married, to a cousin of his from the Uylenburgh family, Magdalena van Loo. Magdalena became pregnant a few months after the wedding, but Titus may never have known it: when she was in her third month, at the latest, Titus died, twenty-six years old. Magdalena, who was the same age as Titus, died seven months after giving birth to a daughter, named Titia after her dead father. If there is any mercy to speak of in this sequence of tragic young deaths, it is that Rembrandt lived to see the birth of Titia and died two weeks before his daughter-in-law, Magdalena—on October 4, 1669, at the age of sixty-three. He lived longer than any of his brothers and sisters, wives and children. It was a life of bright early hope followed by disappointment and bitterness. It was a life that changed the world of art.

CHAPTER EIGHT

~

AFTERLIFE

he story of Rembrandt's life and career tells us a lot about the circumstances under which his art was created, especially the paintings. It tells us how he became famous in his time. But it does not answer our first question: how did Rembrandt become a legend for all time? The answer to that lies in the way he was treated by posterity, in the centuries following his own.

Although Rembrandt's star was in decline when he died, he was still one of the best-known painters of Europe. And he was known for something specific. Certain ways of painting and certain subjects were associated with him. Paintings with deep brown and gray shadows relieved by a single highly lit area are called Rembrandtesque (in the style of Rembrandt). The same word is applied to paintings of dilapidated buildings, poorly dressed old men and women sunk in thought, and nude women with sagging breasts and rimpled thighs. Rembrandt is credited with depicting people the way they really are rather than the way they would like to be or think they should look. He is admired for painting people whose faces give expression to their true feelings and reflect life in all its disappointments.

Posterity also knew—or thought it knew—what Rembrandt was *not*. His art was not elegant, decorative, courtly, or literary. It portrayed the human soul and not the values of organized religion. From what we know about the historical Rembrandt and his work, we can see how these ideas

became attached to him after his death. But we also know that they are not very accurate. Rembrandt *did* work for the court, he was not against making decorative paintings, he had very close ties to the world of literature, and his main aim in painting people was not to show them as naturally as possible. But once labels of this kind get stuck to a reputation, they take on a life of their own. Within a short time after Rembrandt's death, any work of art that matched the clichés were said to be by him.

As long as the world, and the art market, valued elegance above

∾

Jacob Blessing the Sons of Joseph. 1656. **The blind old patriarch Jacob broke tradition by blessing his younger grandson with his right hand. To do this, he crossed his hands, surprising his son Joseph. Rembrandt was intrigued by the unusual Bible story.**

naturalness, Rembrandt was not regarded very highly. Compared with an Italian artist like Raphael, he was considered crude. His character as a person was thought to correspond to his art. The stories about him emphasized his love of money and impoliteness. Still, his art was admired and traded eagerly, if at lower prices than work by Raphael or Rubens.

In the nineteenth century, as ideals of political and social life changed, so did ideas about art. With the decline of the European courts, old standards of grace and beauty began to seem artificial. Nineteenth-century artists looked for true-to-life ways of depicting ordinary human emotions and experiences. When this happened, Rembrandt's art began to look better than it had to more people. The qualities for which it had been put down became cause for praise. As his work rose in value, more paintings and drawings were said to have been by him. "Rembrandtness" was found in thousands of works that had nothing to do with the real Rembrandt.

For the artist's new admirers, it was important to believe that Rembrandt was a sincere person, whose pictures of humanity came from the heart. This was also essential to the Dutch patriots who promoted Rembrandt as a national hero. They erected a statue to him in Amsterdam to rival the statue of Rubens in Antwerp. They put him forward as the greatest Dutch artist of all time, claiming that the stories about his bad character were the result of jealousy and ignorance. Since many early stories *were* fabrications, it was not hard to disprove them. (Few of the documents from Rembrandt's own life were known at the time.)

Rembrandt became a hero of liberals and anti-aristocrats throughout Europe. They saw the seventeenth-century Dutch Republic as a model for the kind of societies they wanted to establish. The art of the republic provided the proof that the lives of ordinary men and women could be glorified—even sanctified—by artists devoted to the real world rather than to the dogmas of the church or the fancies of the courts. Rembrandt was the best example of this. He became nearly a god, worshiped for paintings he did not paint and for human qualities he did not possess.

In the twentieth century, scholars became stricter about defining which works are and are not by Rembrandt. Increasingly, they judge authorship on the basis of technique, style, and quality. Present-day connoisseurs think that these things are more measurable than the mood of a picture and its effect on our emotions. On this basis, more than a thousand paintings and drawings have been removed from the list of Rembrandt's works.

None of this has damaged Rembrandt's artistic reputation any more than it was hurt by the inflated admiration of the nineteenth century. In fact, the reasons given today for Rembrandt's greatness are usually the same ones that were invented in the nineteenth century, even though they are now applied to different paintings.

Apparently, what has made Rembrandt a legend is a combination of ingredients that are not necessarily linked. There are reasons dating back to his own lifetime, such as his prominence from youth onward, his great talent, and his close relations with poets and playwrights who talked and

∾

Long thought to be by Rembrandt, *The Man with the Golden Helmet,* **painted between 1650 and 1660, was by one of his pupils.**

wrote about him. After his death, those who wrote nasty things about him turned him into a symbol of inelegance and boorishness. When those bad characteristics were reinterpreted positively as sincerity and naturalness, his reputation benefited.

These things could have happened to any of the thousands of talented and well-known artists the world has seen, no matter what his or her art was like. In the case of Rembrandt, something else came along. I hesitate to call it artistic quality. That suggests something that can never be taken away, and time and again a painting thought to be by Rembrandt has been cast down when art historians began having doubts about it. A famous example is *The Man with the Golden Helmet,* in Berlin. This canvas was nearly worshiped for seventy years as one of the greatest paintings in the world. But when art historians began doubting whether it was really by Rembrandt or not, the high quality it was first thought to possess somehow faded. There must be something else about Rembrandtesque paintings, aside from their artistic quality, that makes them special.

Without claiming to provide a final answer, I would suggest that Rembrandt's long-lasting fame owes a lot to the fact that it is easy for other artists to copy him or to improvise on his manner. Their adaptations may not have the same quality, but they do have an appealing "Rembrandtness," which adds to Rembrandt's fame when it is made and again when it is unmasked. These works, as well as Rembrandt's originals, have the power to touch people emotionally, since they are about emotions. We react more directly to images of human beings experiencing strong emotions than we do to landscape or history or still life. We feel along with the subjects and allow ourselves to be carried away. When this happens, we say that it is proof of the greatness of Rembrandt's art.

But this is little more than a guess on my part, and your guess is as good as mine. In fact, it is better, because what really sets Rembrandt's art apart is its ability to mean new things to each new generation, and yours is next.

LIST OF ILLUSTRATIONS

PAGES 41–42: *Christ Preaching (The Hundred Guilder Print)*. c. 1643–49. Etching (first state), 10¹⁵/₁₆ × 15⁹/₁₆″. Rijksprentenkabinet, Rijksmuseum, Amsterdam

PAGE 45: Pieter Bast, *Map of Amsterdam*. 1597. Engraving in four sheets, 36⁵/₈ × 32¹/₄″. Historical Topographical Atlas of the Municipal Archives of Amsterdam, The Netherlands

PAGE 46: Peter Paul Rubens, *Christ and the Tribute Money*. c. 1612. Oil on wood panel, 55⁷/₈ × 74³/₈″. The Fine Arts Museum of San Francisco, Museum purchase, M. H. de Young Art Trust Fund

PAGE 47: *The Anatomy Lecture of Dr. Nicolaes Tulp*. 1632. Oil on canvas, 66³/₄ × 85¹/₄″. Koninklijk Kabinet van Schilderijen, The Hague. Photo: © Mauritshuis

PAGES 48–49: Tomas de Keyser, *The Anatomy Lecture of Dr. Sebastiaen Egbertsz. de Vrij*. 1619. Oil on canvas, 53¹/₈ × 73¹/₄″. Rijksmuseum, Amsterdam

PAGE 51: *The Descent of Christ from the Cross*. 1633. Etching, 20⁷/₈ × 16¹/₄″. Rijksprentenkabinet, Rijksmuseum, Amsterdam

PAGE 53 (LEFT): *Saskia*. 1633. Silverpoint on white prepared vellum, 7¹/₄ × 4¹/₄″. Staatliche Museen Pressischer Kulturbesitz, Kupferstichkabinett, Berlin. Photo: Bildarchiv Pressischer Kulturbesitz, Berlin

PAGE 53 (RIGHT): *Saskia*. c. 1634. Oil on panel, 39¹/₄ × 31″. Staatliche Kunstsammlungen, Gemäldegalerie Alte Meister, Kassel

PAGE 54: *Rembrandt and Saskia*. c. 1636. Oil on canvas, 63³/₈ × 51⁵/₈″. Staatliche Kunstsammlungen, Gemäldegalerie Alte Meister, Dresden. Photo: Sachsische Landesbibliothek, Dresden

PAGE 56: Rembrandt-House Museum. c. 1636. Photo: Rembrandt-House Museum, Amsterdam

PAGE 57: *Cornelis Claesz. Anslo and Aeltje Gerritsdr. Schouten*. 1641. Oil on canvas, 69¹/₄ × 82³/₄″. Staatliche Museen Pressischer Kulturbesitz, Gemäldegalerie, Berlin. Photo: Bildarchiv Pressischer Kulturbesitz, Berlin

PAGE 59: *The Risen Christ Appearing to Mary Magdalene*. 1638. Oil on panel, 24 × 19¹/₂″. Collection of Her Majesty Queen Elizabeth II. Photo: Copyright reserved to Her Majesty Queen Elizabeth II

PAGE 64: *The Night Watch*. Detail of figure of Frans Banning Cocq.

PAGES 66–67 AND BACK COVER: *The Night Watch*. 1642. Oil on canvas, 142⁷/₈ × 172¹/₈″. Rijksmuseum, on loan from the City of Amsterdam

PAGE 70: *Hendrickje Bathing*. 1655. Oil on panel, 24³/₈ × 18¹/₂″. The National Gallery, London

PAGE 71: *Young Woman in Bed*. c. 1647. Oil on canvas, 32 × 26³/₄″. National Gallery of Scotland, Edinburgh

PAGE 72: *Andries de Graeff*. 1639. Oil on canvas, 78³/₄ × 48⁷/₈″. Staatliche Kunstsammlungen, Gemäldegalerie Alte Meister, Kassel

PAGE 73: *Jan Six*. 1647. Etching, 9⁵/₈ × 7¹/₂″. The Metropolitan Museum of Art, New York. Bequest of Mrs. H. O. Havemeyer, 1929

PAGE 74: *Six's Bridge*. 1645. Etching, 9⁵/₈ × 8³/₄″. Rijksprentenkabinet, Rijksmuseum, Amsterdam

PAGE 76: *Jan Six*. 1654. Oil on canvas, 44¹/₈ × 40¹/₈″. Six Collection, Amsterdam

PAGE 77: *The Anatomy Lecture of Dr. Jan Deyman* (fragment from the damaged original). 1656. Oil on canvas, 39³/₈ × 52³/₄″. Rijksmuseum, on loan from the City of Amsterdam

PAGE 78: *Titus van Rijn*. 1655. Oil on canvas, 30¹/₄ × 24³/₄″. Museum Boymans-van Beuningen, Rotterdam

PAGE 80: *Jan Antonides van der Linden*. c. 1665. Etching, 4⁷/₈ (image) + 1¹⁵/₁₆ × 4¹/₈″. Fitzwilliam Museum, University of Cambridge

PAGE 81: *The Conspiracy of Claudius Civilis*. c. 1661–62. Oil on canvas, 77¹/₈ × 121⁵/₈″. Nationalmuseum, Stockholm. Photo: Statens Konstmuseer, Stockholm

PAGE 82: *Self-Portrait*. c. 1661–62. Oil on canvas, 45 × 37¹/₂″. The Iveagh Bequest, Kenwood (English Heritage). Photo: English Heritage Photo Library

PAGE 85: *Jacob Blessing the Sons of Joseph*. Detail.

PAGE 86: *Jacob Blessing the Sons of Joseph*. 1656. Oil on canvas, 69¹/₈ × 82⁷/₈″. Staatliche Kunstsammlungen, Gemäldegalerie Alte Meister, Kassel

PAGE 88: A Rembrandt pupil, *The Man with the Golden Helmet*. c. 1650–60. Oil on canvas, 26³/₈ × 23¹/₄″. Staatliche Museen Pressischer Kulturbesitz, Gemäldegalerie, Berlin. Photo: Bildarchiv Pressischer Kulturbesitz, Berlin

INDEX